Christmas in Scandinavia

About the cover

The wood-block designs bordering the cover photograph of the little baker engrossed in preparation of Christmas treats were commissioned by World Book Encyclopedia, Inc., and were hand carved by Robert Borja. Photograph courtesy of the Consulate General of Finland.

Christmas in Scandinavia

Published by
World Book Encyclopedia, Inc.
Chicago, Illinois

Staff

Editor
Jadwiga Lopez

Writer
Corinne Ross

Art Director
William Dobias

Design Director
Ronald Stachowiak

Senior Designer
Bernard Arendt

Photography Director
Fred C. Eckhardt, Jr.

Photo Editing Director
Ann Eriksen

Photo Editors
Marilyn Gartman
Jo Anne M. Ticzkus

The editors wish to thank all those, too numerous to list, who helped with the research for this book. We would like, however, to give special thanks to Liz Christensson, Helen Fletre, Selma Jacobson, and Betty Petroski for their many contributions, and to the Ullestad family of Voss, Norway, for their warm hospitality during the Christmas of 1976.

Contents

Lighting up the dark

Winter in Scandinavia is a gloomy time of darkness and piercing cold. Lakes and streams freeze solid; snow lies heavy on blue-black firs and silver birches, and drifts high against houses. Icicles hang in thick fringes from the eaves, and a warm, brightly lit home offers a welcome haven. From mid-September onward, the days grow ever shorter until the arrival of the winter solstice, around December 22. That is the shortest day of all, the day when the sun is at its greatest distance from the equator.

In pagan times, people believed that the sun turned like a wheel in its annual cycle of the seasons. The Nordic word for Christmas, *Jul* (Yule), is thought to be derived from *hjul*, an older word meaning wheel — probably referring to the midwinter solstice period when the sun "turned" toward springtime, and the new year. Long before Christianity — and Christmas — came to Scandinavia, it was an occasion for jubilant celebration. A great feast was held to hasten the turn of the sun's course, and to honor Freya, goddess of the sun.

A multitude of strange and eerie beliefs filled people's minds in those days. Odin, Frey, Thor, and all the ancient gods of Norse mythology ruled from the palace of Valhalla. Darkness was evil; darkness was the enemy. It was inhabited by goblins, ghosts, witches, and other supernatural beings. No wonder, then, that light — the light of fires, torches, and candles — was always so welcome and necessary, and that Christmas, when it began to be celebrated, was called "the feast of lights."

Christianity arrived in Scandinavia in the 900s, during the era of the Norsemen, or Vikings. Fierce raiders and plunderers, the Vikings sailed their black dragon-prowed ships to many distant lands — England, Ireland, France, Iceland, Greenland, the Mediterranean, even to the northeast coast of America. King Harald Bluetooth, the first Viking to become a Christian, once held a splendid Christmas banquet for 600 men that combined the often violent pagan ceremony of old with elements of his new faith.

After ordering that no sharp-edged implements be used except for the purpose of cutting up meat, he declared Christmas a time of peace. Forty-eight

well-fattened hogs were slaughtered for the occasion, and quantities of beef, mutton, blood-sausages, stews, cabbage soup, bread cakes, fried turnips, and oceans of ale were served. Enlivened by storytelling, the drinking and eating continued for six days!

Since King Harald's time, the Scandinavian countries have acquired many new holiday customs. But traces of the old superstitious dread of the night still survive, and Christmas nowadays celebrates both the promise of diminishing darkness and the Biblical message of peace on earth. It is a mixture of joy and solemnity, and behind almost every light-hearted ritual practiced today lurks a tinge of primitive fear — running like a thread through the years back to the days when people's lives were dependent upon the rhythms of nature, and the whims of long-departed gods and malicious spirits.

The cheerful Nordic custom of energetic house-cleaning, baking, and decorating just before Christmas once had a more serious intent. Everything had to be accomplished before "the peace of Christmas" began, the three-day period of friendliness toward men and beasts that starts on Christmas Eve. Then quiet reigned, lest the spirits be attracted by loud noises or be offended by the sight of someone working. The dead were believed to return at Christmas, too, riding wildly through the night ready to snatch up unwary humans.

The coming of the Christmas season today with its lights, decorations, and traditional foods brings a much needed respite from the rigors of winter and the fervent longing for spring. A feeling of gaiety and good will spreads throughout the countryside. It is a time of well-deserved leisure and fun, of feasting, parties, music and dancing, of visiting friends and relatives — illuminated by glowing candles, firelight reflecting on polished copper and pewter, and fresh flowers — contrasting sharply with the menacing darkness outside.

Each member of the family helps in the preparations, from the oldest to the youngest. Even the birds and animals are not forgotten; everything and everyone is included in the joyous observance of Christmas, oldest of the Nordic festivals . . . the lighting up of the dark.

In ancient times, the sun was often represented as a wheel, or Jul, turning with the seasons. This elaborate wheel-shaped brooch (left) was discovered in Denmark and dates to the Iron Age. Engraving of Thor (lower left), Scandinavian god of thunder. The great hall of Valhalla (below), palace of the gods, where the souls of Viking heroes slain in battle were received.

Lucia's Day

It's very early morning in Sweden, and most people are sleeping soundly. A young girl named Kristin, however, is wide awake and anxiously watching the clock. It is December 13, Lucia's Day, and she is to be Lucia, Queen of Light!

Tiptoeing down to the kitchen, Kristin makes a big pot of coffee and sets a tray with cups and saucers. The day before she had baked lots of special Lucia buns, saffron-flavored, some in the shape of cats' heads. Kristin adds these to the tray, and now everything is ready.

She is dressed in a long white gown, a red sash around her waist. Her blonde hair falls shining to her shoulders — the result of an especially good brushing. Atop her head she places a crown of green leaves and candles. Carefully Kristin lights each candle, then — head held stiffly — carries the laden tray up the stairs to her parents' bedroom. Trying hard not to giggle, she begins to sing.

Father and Mother awake to the sound of a lovely melody, and blink their eyes in astonishment! Flickering candlelight fills the room as a vision in white approaches them. Father sits up and rubs his eyes, then beams with pride. "I thought I was dreaming," he smiles. "But that coffee smells real! Good morning, Kristin — I mean Lucia!"

Through the door behind Kristin burst her little sister and brother; they're too impatient to wait for her to come and wake them, too. Bouncing on their parents' bed they demand their Lucia-cats. Father waits to be served — he knows how important it is for Kristin. Mother waits, too, but the very minute she has finished her coffee and bun she blows out the candles on Kristin's crown. No sense taking chances on singeing her hair.

A wreath of candles on her head, a Lucia Queen (below) leads a procession of attendants and Star Boys at dawn in a Swedish school. Blonde, blue-eyed Lucias wearing whortleberry leaf crowns and carrying lighted candles in celebration of Lucia's Day, December 13 (right).

All over Sweden on this chill winter dawn other Lucia maidens are awakening their families with the same charming ceremony. But the Lucia festival is not just a home celebration. Favorite teachers often receive a surprise morning call, too. Offices and factories have their own Lucias, and hotel guests and hospital patients are visited by candle-crowned young ladies. Even lucky policemen and early-rising streetcar riders are apt to meet a pretty girl in white offering coffee and a bite to eat.

Every parish and village has its special Lucia, and often a parade for her. Sometimes "Star Boys" in tall peaked hats sprinkled with stars accompany the procession, along with riders on horseback and marching groups of young people dressed as Biblical characters, devils, or trolls. In towns and cities, local newspapers sponsor competitions to elect the "Lucia Bride." The winning Lucia of Stockholm, capital of Sweden, parades with nine other beautiful girls, some from Swedish communities all over the world. In gaily bedecked coaches, they drive to City Hall where Lucia is crowned, usually by that year's winner of the Nobel prize for literature.

Many legends are told about the origin of the Lucia festival, but no one knows exactly how it began. The oldest tales date back to pagan days, and might have roots in both the goddess Freya — whose symbols were lights and the household cat — and the winter solstice feast celebrating the return of longer days. Another story tells of a white-robed maiden wearing a crown of burning candles who was said to have brought food to starving villagers in a western Swedish province long ago.

When Christianity came to Sweden, it brought with it a legend from Italy, of a Sicilian girl named Lucia who was condemned to death in A.D. 304 for her Christian beliefs. She was later made a saint, and the Italian air "Santa Lucia" became the traditional song of Swedish "Lucias."

By the old Julian calendar, the winter solstice, longest night of the year, fell on December 13 — also the Christian Saint Lucia's feast day. Somehow the old, pre-Christian Lucia figures and Saint Lucia became entwined, and emerged as one, the living symbol of light to all Swedes. Lucia comes, banishing the winter darkness with her halo of candles, and Lucia's Day announces the official beginning of the Christmas season in Sweden.

A small Lucia maiden proudly carries a breakfast tray with coffee and buns to her sleeping parents.

The
pre-Christmas
whirl

In Norway, at four o'clock on the afternoon of Christmas Eve, church bells peal in "the Christmas peace." But in the preceding days, Norway and all the other Scandinavian countries are caught up in a cheerful furor of holiday preparations. Anything but peaceful, a near-hurricane of cooking, cleaning, and creating tears households apart and puts them back together again — spotless, bright with seasonal trimmings, and redolent with the good smells of Christmas. Children are all abuzz with excitement and bursting with secrets, finishing their gifts and hiding them here and there around the house.

Earlier, in the fall, pigs have been butchered. The pig has always played an important role in Scandinavian Yule festivities. The Vikings considered it the finest meat for holiday feasting, and during the pagan era sacrificed a swine to the gods during their midwinter celebrations, serving it up as the main course later. Nowadays, the remarkable pig is turned into a raft of different products: hams, pork roasts, sausages, cutlets, and headcheese. The feet are pickled, and the head — embellished with pastry decorations, flags, and with an apple in its mouth — is used as a centerpiece.

In rural areas, a truck full of baby pigs arrives sometime in the spring or summer. The children choose one to be "the Christmas pig." They feed and tend it carefully, watching over it with great zeal. At butchering time, however, grown-ups send the youngsters on an errand . . . no one wants to see a pet meet its end. Customarily the men in charge of the butchering all have a drink of aquavit, and may even share it with the one who really needs it — the pig.

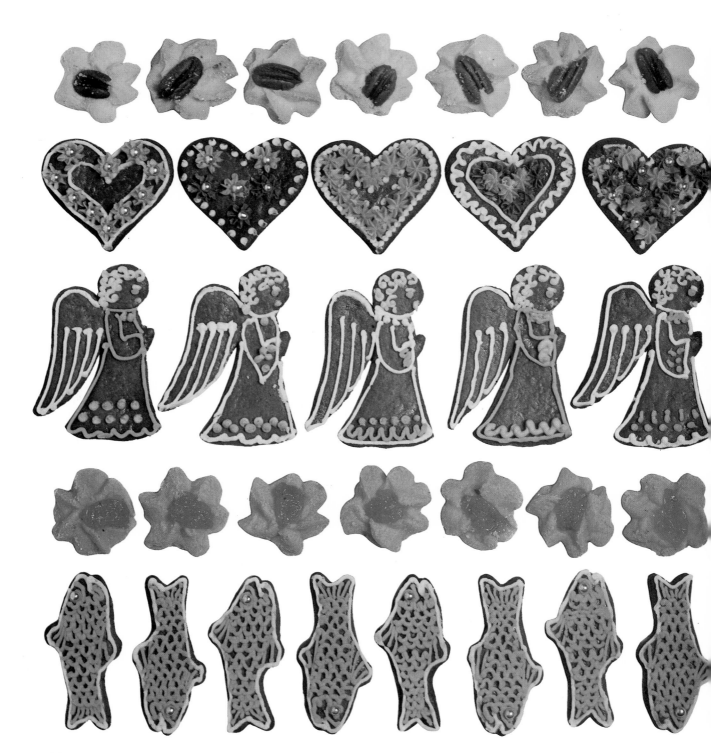

A fury of baking . . .

Scandinavians love good food, and Nordic cooks are second to no one when it comes to baking delicious breads and pastries. Commercial bake-shops offer a profusion of goodies for sale at Christmastime, but many housewives still prefer to serve their own homemade products — and they are well worth the effort.

Tempting odors waft through the entire house as breads are kneaded and baked and trays of cookies are slid in and out of ovens. Cinnamon, saffron, cardamom, candied citron, raisins, currants, nuts — the mouth-watering smells promise fabulous treats to come. Marvelously ornate gingerbread houses are created from cookies, candies, and frosting — lifelike even to cotton puffs of smoke rising from chimneys, frosting icicles hanging from roofs and window ledges, and gingerbread forests nearby.

Christmas cookies are an art form in Scandinavia. There are spicy ginger- and molasses-flavored cookies like *pepparkakor*, and all manner of sugar cookies — formed into cloverleafs, hearts, spirals, stars, pigs, chickens, goats, and goblins. Some — decorated so exquisitely it seems a shame to eat them — become ornaments for the Christmas tree. A good housewife feels duty-bound to produce at least seven kinds of cookies — often as many as fourteen — all to be tucked away in tins awaiting Christmas.

It's a terribly frustrating time for the youngsters. They help mother and grandmother with the baking, but are allowed to eat only the broken fragments. Many people recall that in their youth they were ordered to whistle every time they were sent to the larder where the edibles were stored, so that their mothers would know for sure they weren't sampling the forbidden cakes!

Round rye breads with holes in the middle are baked and strung on a pole hanging from the ceiling; Swedish *vörtbröd* is made from new, unfermented beer; and Norwegian *lefse*, thin bread made of potatoes and flour, awaits the final touches of butter, sugar, honey, or thin slices of brown goat cheese. In Iceland, *laufabraud*, fried cakes cut into designs with a special device, inspire a flurry of competition for the most fanciful shapes. The Finns make a puff pastry with prune filling, called *joulutorttu*.

One method used by old-fashioned cooks to check if the bread was done was to lift it to touch the nose. If the tip of the nose did *not* get burned, the bread was ready. A burned nose meant the loaf had to go back in the oven.

Mother and daughter (left) painstakingly add the finishing touches to a Christmas specialty — the ginger-bread house. Good smells fill the air as children — and a friend — help Mother with the Christmas baking (below).

A frenzy of cleaning . . .

As Christmas draws nearer, wives and daughters begin a merciless cleaning operation. Everything in sight is scrubbed, scoured, polished, or washed. Floors, ceilings, furniture, walls, windows, rugs, cupboards, bedding, linens, utensils — the house is torn up for days as brooms and mops attack any speck of dust that dares to show its face. On the farms, even the barns and stables are invaded.

After the house has been thoroughly purified, the body has its turn, in either a modern bathtub or the *sauna,* a 2,000-year-old tradition in Scandinavia. The sauna is a wooden bathhouse where bathers steam themselves clean, aided by the brisk application of birch twigs. Afterward, the bather cools off with a cold shower, a dash into an icy pond, or even a quick roll in the snow — claimed by all to be very invigorating.

In the old days, after the household was made spick-and-span, straw would be brought in and strewn thickly on the floor. Children played games in it, and everyone slept in it — leaving the beds for those ghostly nighttime visitors who were believed to be abroad at Christmastime. The family even ate amid the straw, but some food and drink would be left on the table for friends or relatives — or ghosts — who might drop in. Although this custom is seldom practiced now, often a handful of straw or branches of fir will be brought in and laid by the door or fireplace, on the mantelpiece, or beneath the table in symbolic commemoration of the ancient ways.

The men were not let off at this time, either. A farmer — besides his regular chores — had to chop enough wood to keep the fires burning through the three days of Christmas peace, when no work was allowed. He might also nail a piece of steel over the door, to prevent trolls from entering the house. Tar crosses were sometimes painted on doors, too, as an added protection against evil spirits.

A flurry of creativity . . .

Just about the only quiet time in the pre-Christmas bustle is when everyone in the family gathers together to make ornaments, gifts, and candles. Out come the burned and broken cookie rejects for snacking, and grown-ups may sip a cheering mug of hot spiced wine, or *glögg*.

Homemade items are especially welcome gifts: jams and preserves, candies, and all kinds of baked goods. Some of these will be taken along to elderly relatives or shut-ins in hospitals on the big visiting day, December 26. All the children, even the littlest, join in the fun of making things, both at home and in school. Handmade book ends, embroidered aprons or handkerchiefs, wooden spoons and spatulas, baskets — the finished product may come out a little lopsided and imperfect, but it's always received with great admiration.

Nowadays, candles in all sizes, shapes, and colors are readily available in stores. But in many Scandinavian households the old art of dipping them by hand is still practiced. And as candles are so much a part of Christmas, lots of them are needed. The kitchen is the center of operations, and while the dipping is going on there's little room left for any other activity. Long strips of wood with strings between them rest on chairs, newspapers cover the floor, and pots of melting tallow sit wherever there is space.

Like magic the candles grow, increasing in size with each dipping of the wick. Nordic Christmas candles are usually white, and come in an amazing variety of shapes: simple single tapers, fat or thin; circular with six branches; flat with seven branches, and the extremely difficult to make curved, three-armed candle.

An old superstition said, "Whatever the light of the candles falls upon will be blessed in the coming year." Years ago, people would bring out their cherished silverware and other treasures — even money and clothing — so that the candles could cast their blessing on them.

A farmer would carry the Christmas candle out to the barn, where he would ceremoniously singe the sign of the cross in the cattle's hair to ensure the

animals' good health. Inside the house, a special Yule candle was placed on the table on Christmas Eve. It would be a large one, as it had to burn through that night and all the other nights of the holiday season. Candles in those days were too costly to be burned every day, but having one to light on Christmas Eve was essential. Begging for candles was common, and they were often given to the poor as gifts.

A fantasy of decorating . . .

One final task still remains before the pre-Christmas whirl is done . . . decorating the house. It's no small job, for Scandinavians delight in bright-ening their homes with masses of greenery, orna-ments, candles, and many other holiday touches.

Brilliantly colored woven wallhangings or tapes-tries were among the earliest Christmas decorations, adding warmth and beauty to the stark wooden walls. Gradually these were replaced by paintings and woodcuts, first on linen and later on paper. They were called "Christmas Papers" or "Letters," portraying Biblical, holiday, or fairy-tale motifs. Tacked up in rows, they would often cover an entire room. Today's versions are colorful paper or cloth hangings embellished with Christmas goblins, geese, bells, or snow-covered red cottages.

What started as a simple wooden candleholder will look festive indeed when it is all covered with cut colored paper (top left). *Scandinavian children enjoy making ornaments for the Christmas tree* (bottom left).

Du lyser julens stjärna klar
högt över snöblå slätter

Fir boughs, festooned with red ribbons and pine cones, are carefully arranged throughout the house, bringing in the scent of the forest. Housewives unearth cherished tablecloths and long runners, beautifully embroidered in gay colors and used only at this time of year. Even the Christmas tree stands on a special mat. Father hangs up straw mobiles and wreaths, and grandmother sets out a small manger adorned with twigs, moss, and bits of straw.

Youngsters especially enjoy putting together tiny winter scenes — under the tree, on a tabletop, or in a corner cupboard. There is always a miniature church, a light in its windows, and little fir trees — maybe even a frozen lake made from a piece of mirror.

And there are candles everywhere — in the windows, massed in ranks on the mantel, on the hearth, and set in brightly painted candleholders on tables, all waiting to be lit.

Finally, all is done . . .

The baking is completed, the cleaning finished, and the decorations are up. After the Christmas Eve bath, everybody puts on new or freshly laundered clothes. The hectic weeks of getting ready are over, and at last, Christmas is really here!

A candle burns in every window, lighting up the darkness for any passing friend or stranger — perhaps even the Christ Child. A slash of light falls on the snow from a quickly opened door — showing the way to cheerful warmth, an abundance of good things to eat, and a joyous Christmas welcome.

A sampler of contemporary "Christmas Papers" (left). *A pyramid of burning candles* (right) *is a common Christmas sight.*

Shops, markets, and fairs

"When can we go look at the decorations?" Scandi-navian parents' ears ring with this oft-repeated plea just before Christmas. Sooner or later, they give in. The truth is, they enjoy the yearly outing just as much as the children do!

There's so much to see . . . it's like walking into a giant Christmas card. Garlands of fresh green fir stretch gracefully from lamppost to lamppost, lit by thousands of tiny white bulbs. Fir trees, frosted with snow, adorn window ledges and street corners, and stand glittering with shiny ornaments in every shop. Copenhagen and other large cities erect a spectacular Christmas tree each year in their main squares, attracting crowds of onlookers awaiting the big moment when the lights are first turned on.

Stars and bells, and countless bright red hearts— a unique Scandinavian Christmas decoration— appear on shopping bags, in display windows, and hanging from ropes of pine over the streets. Store windows framed in boughs of fir show off enchanted landscapes of snow and mountains; electric trains race on winding tracks through miniature villages and mysteriously disappear for a brief moment in tunnels. Sidewalks and streets are thronged with people, old and young, all caught up in the sounds and sights and spirit of Christmas.

Small *nisser*, red-costumed Christmas sprites, wink at passers-by from shop windows where they have taken up residence for the season. Big nisser, adults dressed up in long beards and red suits, wander the streets ready to listen to youngsters' fondest dreams of Christmas gifts. Some department stores have a sign, "Children Parked Free," offering parents a place to leave the kids while they shop for some of those much-wanted presents unwatched by eager eyes.

On Stortorget Square in the medieval part of Stockholm, a Christmas market comes to life each year. Old-fashioned Christmas booths offer toys, holiday breads and gingerbread cookies, gaily painted carved wooden birds, dolls, and candies in bright wrappers. There are woven baskets, hand-crocheted snowflakes, and a wealth of other hand-made articles in wood, metal, crystal, and cloth.

Christmas markets and holiday decorations lure shoppers
throughout Scandinavia in December. This Helsinki
street scene (far left) is being watched over by countless
Christmas sprites, Joulutonttu. Swedish street decorations include rows of lighted gingerbread cookie figures
and masses of bright red hearts (above left). A large
straw Christmas goat (above) observes the crowds
thronging an outdoor market in Sweden.

Each year, traditionally, children are allowed to choose one special ornament of their very own . . . and the Christmas market offers a tempting array of selections. So does Skansen, Stockholm's famed outdoor museum. Here men and women dressed in the costumes of their various provinces work at all kinds of crafts, showing visitors how they're made. The results are for sale at the annual Christmas Fair. Scandinavian crafts are renowned the world over for their originality, color, and workmanship, and Skansen displays some of the finest.

Many ornaments are made of straw. Using straw to make decorations is a custom that may be traced to the old belief that the spirit of the grain lived on in the straw even after it was cut, and that it had magic powers. There are dolls, angels, and crosses; intricately woven straw wreaths and starbursts; and crown mobiles to hang over the dining table.

But the most popular figure of all is the Christmas goat of plaited straw, with long horns, bound with red ribbon. The ubiquitous *Julbock* appears in all sizes — and no household would be complete without at least one at Christmastime.

Admiring Christmas displays, nibbling at ginger-bread men, wishing for that shiny red truck, or the smiling doll with yellow pigtails — it's an exciting treat, for everyone. But feet, large and small, get tired, and arms can't hold another parcel. Mother suggests that it's time to go home — for this year.

A marvelously varied array of ornaments — hearts and stars, angels, fish, and shells — all ingeniously crafted from straw (left). The goat as a holiday symbol has a long history — it was Thor's sacred animal, and the giver of Christmas gifts was said to come riding on a goat. Of Swedish origin, the Christmas billy goat has now spread to other Nordic countries (right).

The Danish Christmas plates

For more than 80 years Denmark has been sharing a very special Christmas keepsake with the rest of the world . . . the beautiful blue and white *Jule Aften*, "Christmas Eve" plates, cherished by collectors everywhere.

Long ago in Europe it was the custom of wealthy families to give their servants platters piled high with good things to eat at Christmastime. Even though the platter was most likely a simple one of wood, the servants, having little else of value, began calling the platters "Christmas Plates" and hanging them on their walls. Before long the platters became objects of rivalry and began to be considered desirable gifts all by themselves. More ornate versions appeared, and the habit of dating them was started.

In 1895 the Danish firm of Bing and Grøndahl produced the first porcelain Christmas plate. The Royal Copenhagen Porcelain Manufactory began issuing its own in 1908. Both firms use one of the most difficult ceramic techniques, that of underglaze painting, and designs may be submitted by any employee. After the artist paints his scene, the plate is dipped in glaze, completely obscuring the decoration. When the plate is fired in the kiln, the scene reappears. On Christmas Eve the mold for that year is broken, never to be reproduced.

Over the years the Christmas plates have told the story of Denmark, its people, symbols, traditions, and history. The 1944 design protested the Nazi occupation by showing the "Sorgenfri" Castle near Copenhagen where King Christian X was held prisoner by the Germans. Snow scenes, fairy tales, family gatherings, churches and cathedrals, fishing boats and ships at sea, reflections of Danish Christmas customs — all have been captured forever by the lovely once-a-year Christmas plates.

Collectors' treasures — the lovely blue and white Jule Aften, *"Christmas Eve" plates of Denmark. Since 1895, a new plate has been produced annually, each showing a scene portraying a bit of Denmark's history, traditions, or Christmas customs.*

The Christmas Seal tradition

In 63 countries around the world, many people glue a special seal somewhere on their outgoing Christmas cards. The stickers are the colorful Christmas Seals, and proceeds from their sales go to support the battle against tuberculosis and other diseases in children.

The idea originated in Denmark in 1903 with Einar Holbøll, a postal clerk. The first seal, portraying Queen Louise, was printed a year later, and more than four million were sold. Sweden, Norway, Finland, and Iceland quickly adopted the custom and it later spread to other nations. Jacob Riis, an emigrant social worker and recorder of Danish folklore, introduced the Christmas Seal in the United States. He published a magazine article describing the work of the seals in Denmark and suggested they be tried here. The first American seal was printed in 1907.

Every year in Denmark the new Christmas Seal is eagerly awaited and then plastered in profusion all over Christmas cards and letters. Now printed in sheets of 50, each seal shows a different picture, the whole presenting a complete scene. A cutout by Hans Christian Andersen was the inspiration for the 1975 seals. That beloved writer of fairy tales was also a fine artist, and an expert in making charming silhouette designs. Wherever he went his scissors went, too, to entertain children and grownups alike.

Margrethe, Queen of Denmark, designed the 1970 stickers . . . a delightful story of Christmas preparations in the Castle in the Sky. Small angels busily clean and decorate the rooms; the choir practices Christmas songs as the choirmaster wrings his hands with worry. More angels arrive, bearing lighted candles for the windows, and finally — when everything is ready — an archangel flies up into the highest tower to ring in Christmas with the great bell, as all the bells in the world begin to ring in unison.

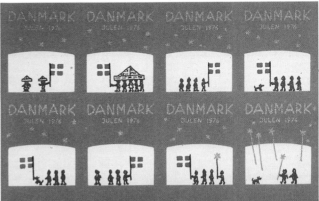

Denmark's Christmas Seals are printed in sheets of 50
that tell a story or present a decorative scene. Hans
Christian Andersen's charming cut-out silhouettes were
the inspiration for the 1975 seals (bottom left). *Angels
in the Castle in the Sky* busily prepare for Christmas
on the 1970 seals, designed by Queen Margrethe II of
Denmark (above).

The Christmas tree

An expedition is afoot. Bundled up in warm clothes, caps, and mittens, a Scandinavian family is about to set out in search of the perfect Christmas tree. The cold air nips at small noses as the children race ahead into the woods on their skis. Father follows along behind, carrying the newly sharpened saw.

Choosing the tree is a serious matter — opinions fly as one tree after another is dismissed with sharp criticism. That one is too tall. This one isn't thick enough. Too short! Father begins to grow a bit impatient when one of the children jumps up with joy and shouts: "Look! Over here . . . this tree has a bird's nest in it!" This, as everyone knows, means good luck, so the matter is settled. Father chops the tree down, the youngsters load it on a sled — nest and all — and the happy group heads home through the crisp snow.

Ever since the days of the Vikings, the evergreen, tree of life, representing immortality and hope, has been the best-loved symbol of the Nordic Yuletide season. In olden times, one particular tree on every farm was honored, especially during the holidays. The farmer might offer it a tankard of beer, poured near the roots. If the tree prospered, so would the farm and the family. Fir trees and boughs were brought indoors and the Yule log, a whole tree stripped of its branches, was hauled inside. One end of it rested in the fireplace, and it would burn throughout the entire holiday season.

But the notion of decorating a tree with ornaments and lights is fairly recent. It began in Germany and then traveled northward to the Nordic countries in the early 1800s. The idea caught on and spread, and today every Scandinavian household has one, as does every store, restaurant, church, hospital, hotel, and public square.

December 23 is usually the day for bringing home the tree. Chopping one's own is the most fun, but if that's not possible there are plenty of cut trees to be had. Small forests suddenly seem to materialize on city street corners and in squares just before Christmas. Tables piled high with fir wreaths, pine cones, cut boughs, and sheafs of wheat line the sidewalks. Outdoor greenhouses are bright splashes of color, filled with fresh flowers of all kinds, cut blooms and in pots.

Once the tree is safely in the house, it will be set up in the middle of the living room. Grown-ups and children both sniff the tangy scent of it with excitement. Decorating the tree, an all-family project, takes place sometime on the day before Christmas.

Lots of the ornaments are handmade, put together during those quiet evenings earlier in the month. Some are heart-shaped baskets of woven paper in gay colors to be filled with candies and nuts. There are carved wooden birds and animals, yarn Christmas gnomes, tiny angels, straw decorations in varied shapes, and intriguing ornaments made of curled wood shavings.

The littlest child reaches high to hang silvered or gilded walnuts and pine cones on a branch — or twisted, glittery icicles and shiny red apples. Big sister adds some of her own frosted cookies, tied on with colored strings. Father tops off the tree — sometimes with an angel, but more often with a large star. Some trees nowadays are lighted with electric bulbs, but real candles are still the most popular illumination. The trees are very fresh, and the candles customarily are lighted only on Christmas Eve, so there's little danger of fire. In Scandinavia, trees are always adorned with national flags, too, perched on a branch or strung over it in long garlands.

Tiny national flags, glittering spiral ornaments, and real lighted candles adorn this Scandinavian Christmas tree (left). Freshly cut from the forest, a tree is carried home through the snow (below).

Boats decorated with garlands of lights for Christmas (top) rest at anchor in an Icelandic port. Laden with Christmas trees, this ship is about to set sail from Stockholm (bottom).

Most Nordic countries have extensive forests of fir — but not Iceland, that land of snowfields, volcanoes, and bubbling hot geysers. The day when the great ships dock with their cargoes of Christmas trees from Norway is awaited with anxious anticipation, and a giant spruce is sent each year to Reykyavík, Iceland's capital. Icelanders sometimes even make their own trees — tying branches of cedar to a wooden framework or perhaps creating the entire tree from painted wood.

Norway also ships a huge tree to London at Christmas where it is erected in Trafalgar Square, a gift from the Norwegian people. It's a custom that began during the German occupation of the 1940s when a spruce was smuggled every year through the German coastal patrols by Norwegian boats to King Haakon, then exiled in England.

Wherever a Scandinavian may be at Christmastime, his thoughts turn to home. If he can he'll travel there via special Christmas ships, trains, or buses. If not, he will celebrate his country's customs as best he can — and the one indispensable item is a tree, even on shipboard. The Nordic countries are seafaring nations, especially Norway, and thousands of men find themselves far from home over the holidays. But the masts of their ships — in harbors or on the ocean — will have a fir tree tied to them.

There are about sixty Scandinavian Seamen's Missions throughout the world, too, and they go all out to provide a homelike holiday atmosphere for homesick sailors. Sometimes it's not easy. The pastor of a mission in Le Havre, France, once decided to celebrate Christmas two and a half months late for a shipload of men who'd been at sea in December. He went out and bought gifts, persuaded townsfolk to write greetings to go with them, and came back triumphantly bearing a tree. It was sadly dried up and brown, but they decorated it anyway, and Christmas was observed with just as much joy as if it had been on time!

Hans Christian Andersen, the Danish storyteller, loved Christmas trees. One of his best-known tales is "The Fir Tree," the story of the small tree that was brought in from the woods and lavishly adorned with every imaginable trinket and ornament. In his autobiography, Andersen recalls the Christmas of 1845, when he happened to be staying in Berlin. His acquaintances all mistakenly assumed that someone else was entertaining him. The famed Swedish singer, Jenny Lind, was also in Berlin, and when she heard that her fellow Scandinavian had been abandoned on Christmas Eve she planned a surprise.

"On the last evening of the year a little tree, with lights and pretty presents, was prepared for me alone — and that by Jenny Lind. The entire circle comprised itself of her, her companion, and me. We three children of the North met together on that Sylvester-evening, and I was the child for whom the Christmas-tree had been lighted up."

*A lighted tree helps bring a touch of holiday gaiety to a
cold and snow-covered dock.*

The goblins
of Christmas

Goblins! Fairy tales are full of them, those small creatures who look like little old men with pointed ears. They have been around for centuries, playing malicious tricks on humans, or—when in the mood —offering a helping hand. At Christmastime in Scandinavia, hordes of them suddenly appear— everywhere—especially in cities.

In Denmark, Norway, and Sweden this annual invasion began about 125 years ago. Before that, the goblins' natural habitat had always been on the farm. In ancient times, farmers believed that the spirit of the land's first settler remained somewhere about, perhaps near his burial mound. This "ancestor" felt that he was still the rightful owner of the land, and it was considered wise to offer his ghost something to eat and drink at Christmas, when the dead were supposed to return.

Later on, the ancestral farm-dweller somehow became mixed up with a goblin-figure called a *nisse*. In Sweden he was known as *tomte*. He lived in the stable, and was capable of causing enormous mischief if crossed. Nisser were typically goblinlike, peevish, and ill tempered. They were the guardians of house and barn, very concerned with the welfare of the farm and the animals. As long as the farmer stayed on good terms with his nisse, all would be well—otherwise, disaster would strike. An almost-full bucket of milk would mysteriously overturn, a harness strap would break, or the cream might sour.

Glædelig Jul

Modern realists state firmly that the nisse is just an imaginary figure. But in the old days many people, particularly the elderly, claimed to have really seen one. And when things went bump in the night on a Nordic farm, it was thought to be a pretty sure thing that it was the nisse, up to some deviltry. On Christmas Eve, to be on the safe side, every family would leave a bowl of rice porridge with a lump of butter in it on the doorstep, or in the barn. In some households, this custom is still practiced today. As the bowl is usually empty by morning, it would seem that the nisse does exist—although nonbelievers still scoff and insist that the cat ate the porridge.

Nisser have long white beards and wear caps, knee breeches, and buckled shoes. Until they began emigrating to cities and towns they dressed soberly in gray, but now they sport festive red or blue costumes. And their names changed, in honor of the holiday. They became *Julenisser*, or Christmas elves, and in Sweden, *Jultomtar*.

Every shop window seems to have several, pretending to be blacksmiths or cobblers, riding toy trains or carts drawn by goats, doing chores, or just grinning back at the faces peering in at them. By the thousands they cavort on Christmas cards and hangings, cling to the branches of Christmas trees, and lurk behind fir boughs on mantelpieces. Julenisser even show up on the labels of Christmas beer bottles and in pots of Christmas plants. And they have become so jovial that sometimes they even play the role of Santa Claus, and bring Christmas gifts.

Santa Claus, our own jolly round-bellied elf in a red suit, also visits some Scandinavian children at Christmas. The legend of Santa, or St. Nicholas, can be traced back to the fourth century, to the story of a bishop in Asia Minor. When St. Nicholas was imported to Scandinavia, he, too, became confused with the ancient farm settler and "nisse" is actually a form of the name Nicholas.

Finland's Christmas elves are called *Joulutonttuja*. They differ from the other Nordic sprites by *always* having been good-natured creatures. They help Santa make toys in his workshop, and spy on children to find out what they want for Christmas. And in Finland, Santa Claus or Father Christmas—whose

A letter from Santa (above). *An early Christmas card* (above right) *shows a gleeful* nisse *with his bowl of Christmas porridge, while the family cat watches hungrily. Two delightful engravings of the nisse* (right): *in one he lights his way in the forest with a lantern* (top), *and in the other* (below) *he warms a bird over a candle flame.*

name in Finnish is *Joulupukki*—delivers the presents.

It's believed in many parts of the world that Santa Claus lives in Lapland, a region of northern Scandinavia and Russia, not far from the North Pole. Great herds of reindeer live there, raised by the Lapps for food and hides. So naturally, there are plenty of them available to help pull Santa's sleigh on Christmas Eve. Every year children from many countries send hundreds of thousands of letters to Santa Claus in Lapland. Each is answered in one of six languages—Finnish, Swedish, German, English, French, or Japanese—all done by volunteers.

Not one, but 13, Christmas goblins come visiting at Christmas in Iceland. They're the *Jola-Sveinar*, or Christmas Boys. Legend has it that they are the sons of Gryla, a gigantic female troll with several heads, 15 tails, goat's horns, ears down to her shoulders, and a beard. The first Christmas Boy arrives 13 days before Christmas. On each following day another comes, and the last appears on Christmas Eve. On Christmas Day the first one leaves, the next day the second, and so on until the sixth of January, 13 days later, when the last one departs.

Originally, the Jola-Sveinar were supposed to be frightening ogres who came down from the mountains at Christmastime and demanded food and other offerings. Over the years the Jola-Sveinar have changed drastically—both in shape and character. In the 1600s they were pictured as giants, in the 1800s as sturdy farmers, and in the 1900s as small, kindly replicas of Santa Claus. They have individual names like Bowl Licker, Door Smeller, Window Peeker, and Skirt Blower—and today the Christmas Boys come bearing gifts.

Christmas is for the birds!

Three pairs of blue eyes stare fixedly through the windowpane of a small farmhouse. Lars has scraped a clear space in the pretty frost patterns covering the glass. Olaf and Helga push closer so they, too, can see out.

In the yard stands a tall sheaf of wheat, saved from the harvest. The afternoon before the children had tied it to a long spruce pole and set it up where they could see it from the house. Now it's Christmas morning, and they are waiting expectantly. The sheaf is their Christmas gift to the birds, and Lars says that the first bird to come will be a red one. Helga, her fingers crossed, hopes for a blue-feathered bird.

Olaf yells with delight! "Look, a whole flock of birds! There's a black and yellow, and a brown—and a red bird, too. Too bad, Helga. I don't see a single blue one."

"It'll come later," Helga retorts. "Anyway, we know the birds like our Christmas sheaf!"

Sharing Christmas with the birds is a very old custom in Scandinavia. Long ago people believed that if large numbers of birds were attracted to the wheat, a year of good crops would be ensured. Sometimes the sheaf is placed on the roof; in Sweden, kernels of corn are often set out on a wheel atop a pole. Some families sprinkle bread crumbs on the snow or in feeders, or tie bits of suet to a small fir tree.

All animals are included in the celebration of Christmas, not just the birds. Farmers give cattle and horses a good brushing and extra portions of oats or barley, along with the greeting: "It's Christmas Eve, good friend; eat well!" Even the fish and game enjoy a holiday respite in Norway—where traps, nets, and snares are removed for the season.

Nordic children wouldn't think of having Christmas without sharing it with the birds. Birds feed happily on a thick sheaf of wheat made up just for them (left). Bound in red, this birds' sheaf awaits its feathered visitors on Christmas morning (right).

From candles
to bonfires

The lighting of one candle . . . in Scandinavia that simple ceremony announces the beginning of Advent, and the start of the Yuletide season. On the first Sunday of Advent, in late November or early December, the first of four candles, in a special candleholder, is lit. It is allowed to burn down a short way, then snuffed out. The following Sunday, both the first candle and the next are lit; on the third Sunday three candles are burned for a brief while. Finally, on the fourth Sunday of Advent, all are set aflame . . . and Christmas is at hand.

Many households also have an Advent wreath, a circlet of pine suspended from the ceiling by ribbons. It, too, holds four candles, one for each of the Advent Sundays. And Advent stars — representing the Star of Bethlehem — glow in many windows, bright with colored lights.

The weeks of Advent fly by only too swiftly for busy grownups; to children Advent means that Christmas is still a long month away. Advent calendars help make the time pass — a little bit. They often appear early in November and are placed in a window or hung on the wall — but — to the children's despair, they're not to be touched until the first day of Advent.

The calendars come in all sorts of shapes and styles, and are sometimes made by the youngsters themselves in school. Some are gay wall hangings with numbered pockets each holding a small gift, or with little trinkets attached by threads or rings all ready to be snipped off, one each day. Most popular, though, are the colorful Christmas scenes on cardboard, with little windows, all shuttered and numbered. Beginning with Advent Sunday, a child may open one window every morning and discover the secret treasure inside — a tiny picture or toy.

Scandinavian Advent calendars come in many sizes and shapes.

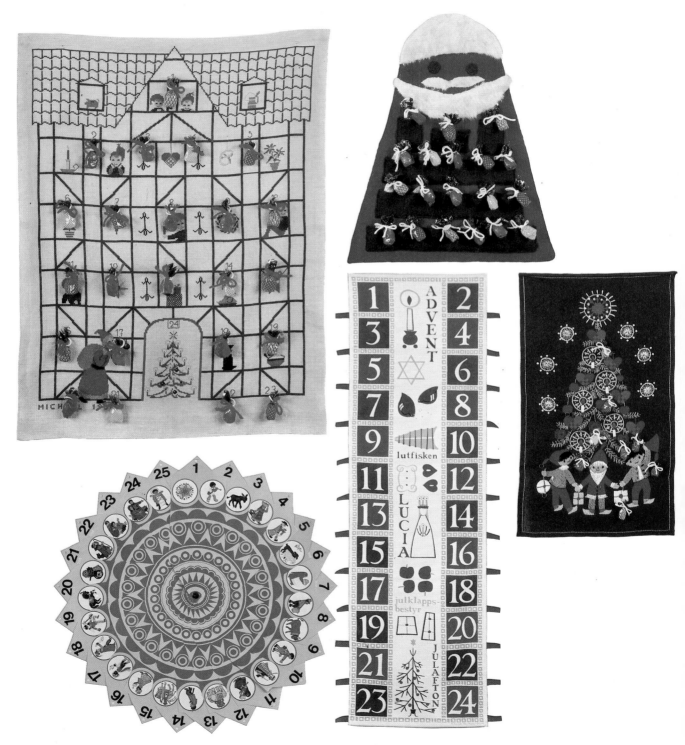

Early Christmas morning service in a lovely old Swedish church (top). A cemetery decorated for Christmas, when it is customary to put flowers and light candles on the graves (bottom).

The first Sunday of Advent in Finland is called "Little Christmas," and it's sort of a dress rehearsal for the real thing. Families exchange gifts, often around a small, decorated tree. Schools present an array of holiday programs for their pupils; business firms and associations entertain staff and members in a whole series of parties, complete with games, merry Santas handing out presents, carol-singing, and dancing.

In all of the Nordic countries, the weeks before Christmas are stuffed full of things to do—shopping sprees, trips to admire holiday decorations and lights, visits to confectioners' shops for marzipan animals and fruit, and to stores bursting with gifts, toys, and books. Households are all adither with feverish cleaning and baking, and giggling conferences are held with great secrecy as children work at composing little rhymes to go with their gifts.

An old saying goes: "Christmas lasts a month in Sweden," and so it does. The festivities there begin on December 13, Lucia's Day, and end exactly one month later, on January 13—St. Knut's Day. Many Nordic homes hold another preview of Christmas on December 23rd, "Little Christmas Eve." That's when the tree is set up and decorated, and it's also the time to celebrate for those unlucky souls who won't be able to be there on Christmas itself.

But it's on the 24th, Christmas Eve, that the activities reach a climax. The birds' sheaf is placed outside, baths are taken and fresh clothes put on. Some people wear traditional costumes, embroidered in bright colors. The table is set with immaculate holiday runners and the best dishes and silver, and the house is filled with masses of candles, greenery, and flowers. Especially flowers—in the long, long winter night of Scandinavia, living flowers in a multitude of colors and smelling sweetly of spring are particularly welcome. Down from attics come clay pots of flowers carefully forced into early bloom; florist shops and outdoor flower markets almost overflow with cut flowers, potted hyacinths and crocuses in blue and purple, white lilies of the valley, tulips in rainbow colors, and pink *Julegleder*, "Joys of Christmas."

53

All tasks must be completed by late afternoon, when the church bells set up a steady pealing, and the peace of Christmas begins. People flock to church to pray and sing the ancient hymns amidst the golden light of hundreds of candles, on altars, attached to pews, and on Christmas trees. It's customary, also, on Christmas Eve, to pay a visit to the cemetery. Flowers, and candles protected by glass cylinders or set in hollow snowballs, are placed on the graves of relatives and the dead of World War II. It's an unforgettable sight — the flickering flames of many candles against the whiteness of the snow, here and there a glowing red tulip placed lovingly on a grave, lacy snowflakes falling gently down through the dusk. And then it's home again . . . and Christmas commences.

Doppa i grytan, "dipping in the pot," is a unique Swedish Christmas Eve custom. It stems from a famine winter many years ago when the only food available was thin broth and black bread. Everyone in the family troops out to the kitchen where the liquid left after boiling the ham and sausage is simmering in a large pot on the stove. Each dips a chunk of dark rye bread into the steaming broth and eats it — as a token of good luck for the coming year.

A vast smörgåsbord of marvelous things to eat — that's the Scandinavian Christmas Eve table! There'll be a large, beautifully decorated ham for the main course, except in Denmark where roast goose stuffed with apples and prunes and adorned with small Danish flags is favored. The Danes also forgo the ritual *lutfisk*, an absolute must in other Nordic countries. Dried ling soaked in lye, then rinsed many times to get rid of the taste and smell, lutfisk miraculously arrives at table boneless and steamed fluffy, to be served with melted butter, white sauce, and boiled potatoes.

And . . . there may be platters of smoked mutton, pork ribs, and pickled herring, herring salads, jellied veal, marinated cucumbers, spicy sausages, liver paté, red cabbage, mashed turnips, assortments of cheeses, bountiful selections of breads, and hordes of delicious Christmas cookies — perhaps twenty or thirty different offerings all waiting to be sampled.

Somewhere amidst all this plenty a rather humble

It's Christmas Eve, and a little boy (above) *eagerly opens a handsomely wrapped present. Old Danish engraving* (right) *portrays a family dancing 'round the tree on Christmas Eve.*

dish appears — a Scandinavian Christmas specialty — rice porridge. It may be served at the start of the meal or as dessert, but it's always included. There's much laughter as each person makes up an obligatory rhyme before tasting the porridge, and somewhere, hidden inside someone's portion, there will be an almond. Whoever finds it is supposed to get married during the coming year. For those already wed, or too young to think about such things, the almond means good luck — and the finder usually receives a small gift, too — maybe a fat marzipan pig with a red ribbon around its neck.

Children often are observed to be suffering from a strange lack of appetite at Christmas Eve dinner. They know that when the grownups *finally* stop eating, then and only then will it be time for the tree ... and the presents. Sometimes they're allowed to open just one present ahead of time, as a reward for being so patient about waiting. At some point Father sneaks away, trying not to be noticed, and lights the candles on the tree. At last! With a great to-do, Father flings open the living room doors, and there it stands — the Christmas tree!

Real candles all alight, its branches bedecked with flags, ornaments of glass, straw or paper, cookies and candy-filled baskets, the tree is reflected in all its glory in the wide, wide eyes of the children. Linking hands, the entire family circles around the tree, singing carols. Father calls for silence, and when he has everyone's attention, reads the old, familiar Christmas gospel.

In Finland, children anxiously await a sharp knock on the door — and in comes Father Christmas with his bulging sack. "Are there any good children here?" he asks. Each child is questioned — even older youngsters can't help feeling a twinge of pleasurable fear as they reply "yes!" — trusting that their parents will agree.

In other Nordic households Father, or maybe Uncle Eric, disguises himself as Julenisse or Jultomte — or maybe Santa Claus — and deals out the gifts. The littlest kids firmly believe he's the real thing; teen-agers enjoy guessing whose face is behind that long white beard.

Long ago in Sweden gifts were known as *Julklappar*, or "Christmas knock." In those days the big presents were given at New Year's and the Christmas gift was only a token, usually something silly. The bearer, often a young boy dressed up as a Christmas goat, would knock on the door, then enter and chase everybody around the room. The make-believe goat would throw his gift onto the floor, and Father, grabbing him by the horns, would rush him briskly back out the door. Later the boy would return, without his costume, and pretend to be greatly surprised to hear that the Christmas goat had already been there.

Gifts are opened one at a time, so everyone can enjoy them to the fullest. In many families it's the custom to attach a card to each present with a rhyme written on it. It is, whenever possible, in the form of a riddle, hinting of the contents or poking fun at the foibles of the recipient. The verses, which have taken many long hours to compose, are read aloud and the person tries to guess what's inside. In a large family, all of this takes a lot of time, and it may be quite late before everybody gets to bed.

Christmas Day is a quiet family affair, a good thing after such a busy night. Stores, theaters, museums, most restaurants, and even some hotels are closed. Many people attend *Julotta*, the solemn early church service, held perhaps in an ancient wooden stave church built during the Middle Ages. In the country some still drive to church through the darkness of the silent forests in sleighs jingling merrily with silver bells, carrying torches which are tossed onto a huge bonfire outside.

Once, the torches were meant as a protection against all the supernatural beings abroad at Christmas ... Every cottage along the route would have candles burning in its windows to help light the way and someone had to stay home to mind the candles while everybody else was in church. After church was done, farmers in those days competed with one another in a wild race homewards because the first man to reach his farm would be the first to have his harvest in.

Even today, horse-drawn sleighs race through the dark, snow-covered woods early on Christmas morning on their way to church, blazing torches lighting the way.

Laden with good things to eat—a Danish Christmas dinner table (above). St. Stephen's Race as shown in an engraving by Clause Magnus (top right). The "Yule Pile" (below right), a stack of Christmas breads and cookies topped by a shiny apple—a traditional Christmas morning treat for children.

In some parts of Denmark, at sunrise on Christmas Day, the town musicians "blow in the Yule," climbing steep ladders to the belfry of the church and playing four hymns, one to each corner of the compass. When they're finished, all the church bells are rung.

Back home again, it's time for Christmas breakfast, an informal but sumptuous spread of meats, cheeses, fish, breads, and sweets. Each child may have his own special "Yule pile"—a stack of loaves, buns, and cookies, topped by a shiny red apple, for nibbling on in private. In olden times the Christmas table, once set, was never cleared as long as the holiday season lasted. "I look forward to Christmas to be able to eat during the night," was a favorite Finnish saying throughout the year. The remainder of Christmas Day is spent snacking, playing with toys, reading new books, or napping.

December 26 is a legal holiday, and is called "Second Day Christmas." It is also St. Stephen's Day— the feast day of a Christian missionary, once a stable boy, who came to Sweden around A.D. 1050. "Staffan Boys" held swift races on this day in years past, riding their horses as fast as they could go to a brook, spring, river, or watering trough. The first horse to drink was supposed to be healthy and vigorous in the months to come. Later, Staffan's ride changed to a sort of procession, the riders wearing disguises and visiting farms along the way. They would sing as they begged for money and food for a holiday party of their own. Staffan Singers still exist today, usually students dressed in costumes and carrying lanterns as they ride through the streets singing their traditional songs and asking for contributions.

Up to this point the holiday observances have been pretty much centered around the home in most of the Nordic countries. Second Day Christmas initiates a new phase—of visiting, trying out new skis and sleds out of doors, and lots of parties, dancing, and music. December 26 is the traditional day to go see shut-ins and people in hospitals, bearing flowers and a packet of Christmas food—candy, cookies, buns, and sometimes even a morsel of lutfisk or a bowl of rice porridge. Paying calls on friends is customary, too, and one must always accept something to eat . . . it's said that if you don't, "You will

The special Christmas parties for children are often enlivened by entertainment. Puppet shows, like this one from Iceland, are perennial favorites.

walk out and take Christmas with you.''

Families gather together with all the aunts, uncles, and cousins joining the children in games and song, and young people recite a popular verse that goes: ''Christmas is here again, and Christmas will last till Easter — but this cannot be so, for in between comes Lent.'' Schools, clubs, unions, civic organizations, businesses and factories amuse children with afternoon entertainments. The kids have a grand time watching puppet shows and pantomimes, eating ice cream and cake, and inevitably there'll be a Santa or other Christmas figure handing out gifts beside a Christmas tree. At night the grownups have their own parties, or attend the theater.

Norway and Denmark have a holiday custom called *Julebukking*. Julebukk is our old friend, the Christmas goat, and years ago a trio of young men would go about pretending to be the beast, threatening people with mischief if the Yule rules weren't observed. One held a long pole with a goat's head at the end, another made the jaw move by pulling a string, and the third rode the ''goat.'' They'd call at various houses, sometimes several of them banding together, and try to scare the children. If one of the ''goats'' was recognized, he'd have to leave — unless expressly asked to stay.

Julebukker nowadays chastise misbehaving children by butting them, and if one goat should meet another, they stage a mock battle. In most areas, Julebukking has become more of a Halloween style trick-or-treating. Groups of children, masked and disguised in fanciful outfits, go from house to house asking for treats, for which they sing in return.

The next major celebration is New Year's Eve. Restaurants are jammed, there are parties everywhere, and city streets swarm with people. At midnight ships' whistles and fog horns blast off in every harbor, church bells toll, and fireworks explode with noisy exuberance. The fireworks are not planned civic events — families have their own, and the night resounds with whooshing rockets and popping firecrackers. In rural areas people still shoot off rifles and set up a clamor by banging on metal pots and pans . . . once this was intended to scare off evil spirits, but now it's just for fun.

Star Boys walk in procession singing their traditional songs.

The start of the New Year is, traditionally, a time for thinking about the future, and the Scandinavian people have long believed in omens, good and bad, concerning it. An old Swedish superstition said that you must not quarrel on New Year's morning, or you would quarrel the whole year. In Finland it's still a common practice to pour molten tin into a bowl of cold water and then try and predict the future from the shapes assumed by the hardening metal.

An unusual tradition in some parts of Denmark is to save cracked and broken crockery during the year for New Year's Eve, when it's tossed against the door of a favorite friend. The thrower then runs — but not too far, as the idea is to be caught and invited in for something to eat! It is also easy to see who is the most popular person in town — by the amount of crockery piled up against the door next morning.

January 6, Twelfth Night, signals the last of Christmas in Denmark, Finland, and Iceland. It's the occasion for a final party and the discarding of the Christmas tree. In most of the Scandinavian countries Twelfth Night brings the Star Boys, singing carols as they walk their rounds. White-robed, wearing conical hats, the youngsters dress up as Biblical characters and carry lighted paper stars mounted on poles. Among them will be the Three Kings, Herod, Judas, and often a Christmas goat. The first Star Boys date back to medieval times when scholars would present Nativity plays on Lucia's Day or later during the Christmas season. They were usually poor and the money they received went to pay for their tuition — or sometimes, like the Staffan Singers, they would ask for food for a party.

Norway and Sweden wind up their Yuletide season on January 13, St. Knut's Day — 20 days after Christmas. "Twentieth-day Knut drives Yule out," proclaims an ancient verse, and in the old days Christmas was literally swept from the house as windows and doors were thrown open, decorations torn down, and everything was swept clean. Crying "Out goes the Yule!" the family went about knocking on the walls with sticks — and any stubborn nisse, ghost, troll, or other spirit still hanging around went flying.

Nowadays it's the children who really celebrate Knut's Day, with as many parties as they can manage to attend. Most of the festivities take place around the Christmas tree — and sometimes there'll be a small tree just for the kids. All valuable or breakable ornaments are removed from the tree ahead of time, but it's still well-laden with cookies, candies, apples, and nuts. Hand-in-hand the youngsters dance one last time around the tree, and then — with shouts of glee — they fall upon it, plundering it of all the goodies.

Now the Christmas tree is ready to receive its final homage . . . as it's tossed onto a pile of other firs and set aflame as part of an enormous bonfire. It is a fitting finale to Christmas in Scandinavia, where Yuletide begins with the lighting of a single candle and ends in a fiery spectacle of blazing pine — both symbolizing the never-failing triumph of light over the darkness.

Christmas trees blaze in a mighty bonfire — a spectacular ending to Christmas in Scandinavia.

For a joyous Scandinavian Christmas...

On the following pages, you'll find a collection of easy-to-make projects, delicious recipes, and songs to sing to help you and your family create an authentic Scandinavian Christmas.

Simple-to-follow directions tell you how to make charming Scandinavian tree decorations — colorful candy rolls filled with goodies and paper baskets in the shape of hearts. There are Santas to cut out or make from spools, and ornaments of straw to use on the tree or anywhere throughout the house. And you can even dip your own Christmas candles following our step-by-step instructions.

From the five different countries covered in this book, we have chosen a sampling of typical holiday recipes. In keeping with the Scandinavian traditions, they include lots of good things to bake — Lucia buns, Icelandic Christmas cake, and several varieties of cookies.

When all is ready, gather your family hand-in-hand around the tree and sing the beloved traditional melodies of Scandinavian Christmas. And so you can properly wish everyone Merry Christmas, here's the way it's said in the Scandinavian countries —

Norway and Sweden: "God Jul"
Denmark: "Glædelig Jul"
Finland: "Hyvää Joulua"
Iceland: "Gleðileg Jól"

Straw ornaments

Star A. Use stalks of either rye or oat straw. The straw must be kept damp overnight so it will bend easily. Use bright red embroidery thread for tying the straw. Cut ten 7-inch long pieces of straw. Tie them together in the middle with a very tight knot. Always wrap red thread around the straws twice before tying them. Take four of the straws and tie them $\frac{1}{2}$" from the center. Repeat five times. Tie the two middle straws together $\frac{1}{2}$" above the last knot. Tie points of star together as shown in figure 4.

Star B. Cut five straws, each 7" long. Tie them together 2" from the top. Take five more straws, 3" long, and tie them in the middle. Attach the two parts together where they are tied, laying the long straws vertically, and the short ones horizontally. Leave enough thread for a hanging loop. Trim with razor blade to obtain a star as shown in figure 3.

Star C. Flatten four 3-inch long, two 4-inch long, and two 2-inch long pieces of straw. Form a square with the four shorter pieces of straw and place the longer ones diagonally inside the square. Tie the six pieces together in the four corners. Leave enough thread to form a loop for hanging. Weave the two 2-inch pieces crosswise in the center of the star. Cut ends as shown in figure C.

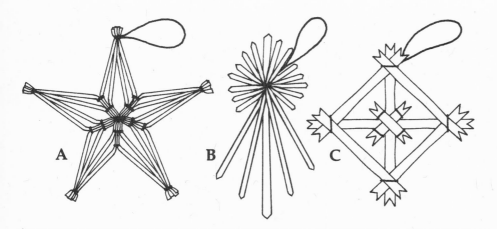

A   B   C

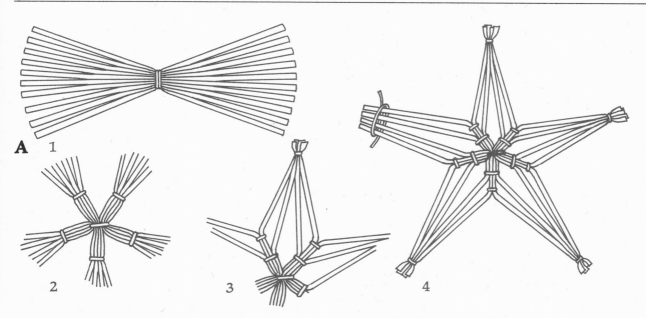

A   1

2   3   4

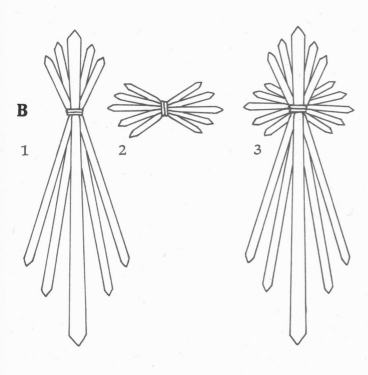

B

1   2   3

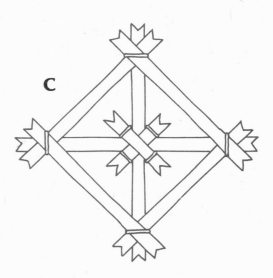

C

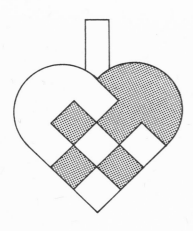

Christmas heart baskets

1. Fold two 3" x 8" pieces of paper of different color in half.

2. Using a pencil, lightly draw a dotted line 1" from the unfolded end of each rectangle. Round off the rectangles above this line to form arch shapes.

3. Cut two slits 1" from the sides of each arch up to the dotted line, dividing both arches into three equal strips.

4. Weave the three strips of each arch through each other to form a heart shape.

5. Open up the basket to smooth out the weave and glue a ½" x 5" strip of colored paper to form a handle. Fill the basket with nuts and candies.

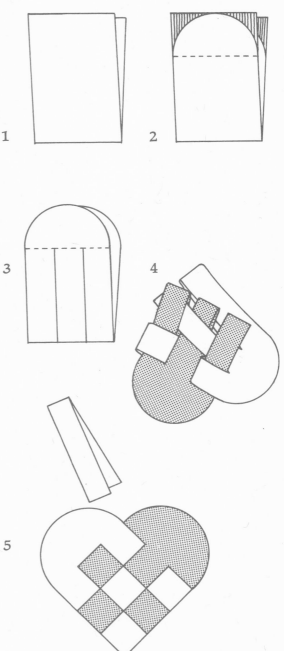

Christmas candy roll

1. Cut a piece of thin cardboard, approximately 4" x 7". Roll it until the edges overlap about $\frac{1}{2}$"; tape or glue it, forming a tubular shape. Fill with candies. Close the ends with tape.

2. Using tissue paper in two different colors, cut four 4" x 8" pieces. Fold lengthwise. Starting from the folded edge, cut slashes, approximately $\frac{1}{4}$" apart, to within $\frac{1}{2}$" of the unfolded edge.

3. Unfold fringe and turn it inside out.

4. Attach fringe with tape or glue to one end of the roll and start winding it around in such a way that only the fringe is visible. Wind two pieces of fringe on each end, alternating the colors. Leave an area of about 2" in the middle of the roll uncovered.

5. Decorate uncovered center with shiny wrapping paper. Glue a small Christmas picture in the middle. Attach a thin string or paper ribbon for hanging.

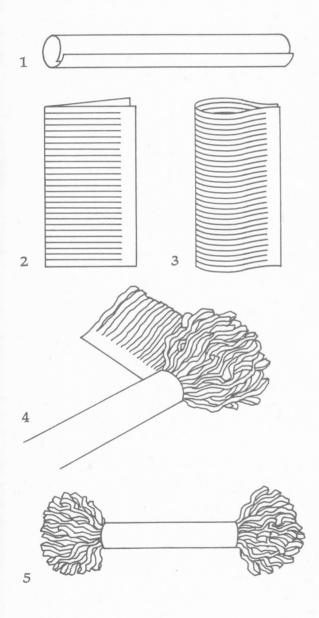

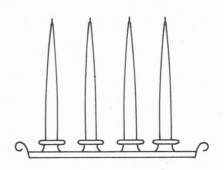

Candles

Prepared candle wax and wicks are available at hobby shops. The candle will burn better if you add about 2 ounces of natural beeswax to each pound of candle wax. One pound of wax makes about six candles. The wicks should be cut in lengths of 15". Tie three wicks on a wooden stick, $\frac{1}{2}$" x $\frac{1}{2}$" x 18" long. Make a knot at the other end of each wick. The wicks should hang at least 3" apart. Place two high-backed chairs, with backs facing, about 6' apart. Lay 2 one by ones across the chairs, 14" apart. Cover the floor with old newspapers.

Melt candle wax and beeswax in a metal bucket, at least 13" high. Add hot (160° F) water until the bucket is almost filled. The wax will float to the top. Dip the three wicks with a smooth movement to the bottom of the bucket. Count to three, then pull out the wicks and hang them on the rack between the chairs. Let the candles cool, then dip them again. After four dippings, the candles should be straightened out with the fingertips. If wax is building up on the bottom, trim it with a knife or scissors. Continue this procedure until candles are the desired thickness (an average-size candle might require 15 to 25 dippings). Add more hot water to the melted wax as needed.

Let the candles hang a few hours before using or storing them, but trim off any unevenness while still warm. Candle wicks should be about $\frac{1}{2}$" long.

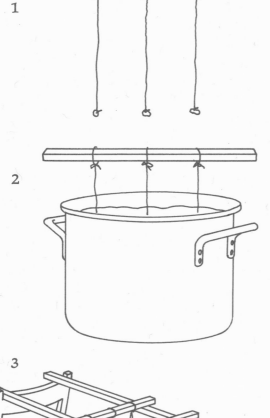

1

2

3

Cutout Santas

These cutout Santas make a decorative centerpiece. Trace the Santa pattern (fig. 1) on red construction paper of desired length. Accordion pleat the paper every $2\frac{1}{2}''$. Cut the pattern out with pointed scissors, making sure that all the Santas are connected by hands, hats, and by the standing base as shown (fig. 2). Partly unfold the paper to make the chain of Santas stand.

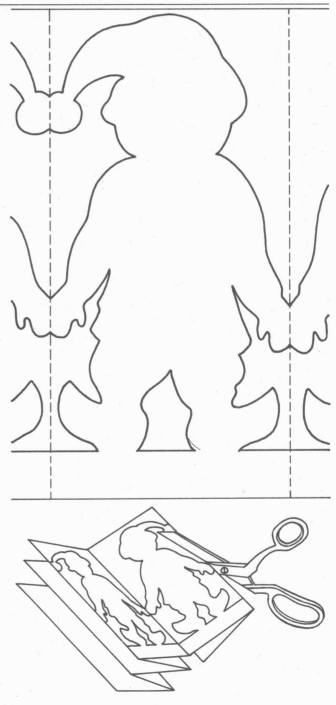

Things to eat

Pickled herring

2 salt herrings (1 to 1½
  pounds each), cleaned
  and cut in fillets
3 quarts cold water
1 large onion
1 cup cider vinegar
1 cup water
1 bay leaf
1 tablespoon
  peppercorns
Parsley sprigs

1. Put herring and cold water into a large bowl. Set aside to soak 3 hours, then drain and cut into pieces (about 2″ square).
2. Slice onion and separate into rings. Place a layer of herring into a shallow bowl and top with some onion rings. Repeat layering of herring and onion rings.
3. Combine vinegar, water, bay leaf, and peppercorns. Pour over herring and onion. Chill thoroughly in refrigerator several hours or overnight for blending of flavors.
4. When ready to serve, drain off liquid. Toss herring and onion gently to mix and put into a serving bowl. Garnish with parsley.

   10 to 12 servings

Roast goose

1 goose (8 to 10 pounds)
1 tablespoon salt
¼ teaspoon black pepper
1 pound cooking apples,
  pared, cored, and
  quartered
12 ounces prunes,
  cooked, drained, and
  pitted
1 tablespoon sugar
Salt

Gravy:
2 cups hot water
½ cup cold water
¼ cup flour

1. Rinse goose and remove any large layers of fat from cavities. Pat dry and rub both cavities with a mixture of the 1 tablespoon salt and the pepper.
2. Mix apples, prunes, and sugar; lightly spoon mixture into body and neck cavities. Close body cavity with skewers or stitches. Fasten neck skin to back with skewer. Loop cord around legs and tighten slightly. Rub skin of goose with a little salt. Place, breast side down, on a rack in a shallow roasting pan.
3. Roast at 325° F. for 2½ hours; remove fat from pan frequently. Turn goose, breast side up, and roast 45 to 60 minutes longer, or until goose tests done (drumstick-thigh joint moves easily). Transfer goose to a heated serving platter or carving board. Garnish as desired.
4. To make gravy, remove all but ¼ cup of drippings from roasting pan. Add hot water; heat to boiling, stirring to loosen browned residue. Stir in a mixture of cold water and flour. Boil 1 to 2 minutes, stirring constantly. Season to taste.

   About 8 servings

Lucia buns

2 packages active dry
   yeast
$\frac{1}{2}$ cup warm water
   (105°-110° F.)
1$\frac{1}{2}$ cups warm milk
   (105°-110° F.)
1 cup sugar
$\frac{3}{4}$ cup butter, cut in
   pieces and softened
1 egg, slightly beaten
$\frac{3}{4}$ teaspoon salt
$\frac{1}{4}$ teaspoon saffron
6$\frac{1}{4}$ cups all-purpose flour
   (more if needed)
Raisins
1 egg yolk
2 teaspoons water

1. In a large mixing bowl, combine yeast and warm water; stir until dissolved. Blend in warm milk, sugar, butter, egg, salt, and saffron. Stir in enough flour to form a stiff dough.
2. On a lightly floured board, knead dough until smooth and elastic (about 10 minutes). Add flour as needed to prevent dough from sticking.
3. Place dough in a greased bowl; turn dough over to grease top. Cover and let rise in a warm place until double in bulk (about 1 hour).
4. Punch down dough, turn out onto a lightly floured board, and knead gently. Pinch off balls of dough about 1$\frac{1}{2}$" in diameter. Roll each ball into a smooth rope about 12" long. Place on a lightly greased baking sheet and form desired shapes (see below), using raisins as indicated.
5. Cover and let rise in a warm place until almost double in bulk (about 25 minutes). Beat egg yolk with water and brush over buns.
6. Bake at 375° F. for about 20 minutes, or until golden-brown. Remove to wire racks. Serve warm or cool.

   4 to 5 dozen single buns

   Single S buns (Christmas boar): Coil ends of each rope in opposite directions, forming an S shape. Place a raisin in the center of each coil.

   Double S buns (Christmas goat cart): Form two S shapes as above, laying one across the other to form a cross.

   Triple S buns (Christmas wagon): Form three S shapes as above, crossing each other at center.

Poor Man's cookies

10 egg yolks
2 egg whites
¾ cup sugar
3 tablespoons brandy
1 cup whipping cream
1 teaspoon ground
  cardamom
5 cups flour (more if
  needed)
Oil or lard for deep-
  frying heated to 365° F.
Confectioners' sugar

1. In a large bowl, beat egg yolks, egg whites, sugar, and brandy until light. Beat in cream and cardamom, then fold in enough flour to make a soft dough. Wrap and refrigerate overnight.
2. Roll out dough, a small portion at a time, on a floured surface to about $\frac{1}{16}$-inch thick. Using a pastry cutter or sharp knife, cut dough into 5" x 2" diamond shapes. Make a lengthwise slit in the center of each diamond, pull one tip through the slit, and tuck the tip back under itself.
3. Deep-fry only as many cookies at one time as will float uncrowded one layer deep in oil. Deep-fry 1 to 2 minutes, or until golden-brown, turning once.
4. Drain cookies over oil a few seconds before removing to absorbent paper. Sift confectioners' sugar over warm cookies. Store in tightly covered containers.
   About 6 dozen cookies

Danish peppernuts

4 cups flour
1 teaspoon crushed
  ammonium carbonate
  (available at a
  pharmacy)
1½ teaspoons ground
  cinnamon
1 teaspoon white pepper
1 teaspoon ground ginger
¾ cup butter
4 teaspoons finely
  shredded lemon peel
1¼ cups sugar
2 eggs
¾ cup finely chopped
  almonds

1. Blend flour with ammonium carbonate and spices; set aside.
2. Cream butter with lemon peel. Add sugar gradually, beating until fluffy. Add eggs, one at a time, beating thoroughly after each addition. Stir in almonds.
3. Add dry ingredients, a third at a time, mixing until blended after each addition. Chill dough about 1 hour.
4. Shape into 1¼-inch balls and place on ungreased cookie sheets.
5. Bake at 350° F. for 12 to 15 minutes, or until tops are very lightly browned. Cool on wire racks.
   About 6 dozen cookies

	Gingerbread cookies	
1 cup sugar		1. Combine sugar, molasses, butter, and spices in a large saucepan. Heat to boiling, stirring occasionally. Remove from heat and stir in baking soda and salt. Cool to lukewarm. Stir in eggs and gradually mix in flour. Chill overnight.

1 cup sugar
1 cup light molasses
1 cup butter
2 teaspoons ground ginger
1 tablespoon ground
  cinnamon
1 teaspoon ground cloves
1 tablespoon baking soda
½ teaspoon salt
2 eggs, slightly beaten
4¾ cups flour

Gingerbread cookies

1. Combine sugar, molasses, butter, and spices in a large saucepan. Heat to boiling, stirring occasionally. Remove from heat and stir in baking soda and salt. Cool to lukewarm. Stir in eggs and gradually mix in flour. Chill overnight.
2. Roll out fourths of the chilled dough thinly on a lightly floured surface, using as little flour as possible. Cut dough into desired shapes with floured cookie cutters. Place on lightly greased cookie sheets.
3. Bake at 375° F. for 5 to 7 minutes. Remove cookies to wire racks; cool.
   About 15 dozen cookies

⅔ cup butter (at room
  temperature)
1 cup sugar
5 eggs
1⅔ cups flour
½ teaspoon baking
  powder
½ cup chopped dates
½ cup seedless raisins
⅔ cup semisweet
  chocolate bits

Icelandic Christmas cake

1. In a large mixing bowl, beat butter and sugar until creamy and light. Add eggs, one at a time, beating well after each addition.
2. Mix flour with baking powder and stir into butter mixture. Stir in dates, raisins, and chocolate bits. Turn batter into a greased 9-inch tube pan and spread evenly.
3. Bake at 375° F. for about 45 minutes, or until a wooden pick inserted into the cake comes out clean.
4. Remove from oven and invert pan on a wire rack to cool for 10 minutes. Remove from pan and cool completely on wire rack. Wrap and store a day before cutting.
   One 9-inch tube cake

2 bottles (26 ounces
  each) burgundy
1 bottle (26 ounces)
  aquavit or gin
¾ cup raisins
½ cup sugar
1 tablespoon cardamom
  seeds
½ teaspoon cloves
Stick cinnamon (3½" long)
1 strip lemon peel (3" x 1")
Raisins
Blanched whole almonds

Christmas wine punch

1. Pour burgundy and half of aquavit into a large saucepan. Stir in ¾ cup raisins and the sugar. Tie spices and lemon peel in cheesecloth and drop into wine mixture.
2. Cover and bring very slowly to boiling; simmer 30 minutes. Add remaining aquavit. Remove from heat and take out spice bag. Ignite mixture in saucepan.
3. Ladle hot mixture into punch cups or mugs, placing some raisins and almonds in each cup.
   About 1½ quarts punch

Carols to sing

Now It Is Christmas Time

Swedish Folk Song
Arranged by Marie Pooler
English version by Frank Pooler

From *Christmas, An American Annual of Christmas Literature and Art*, Vol. 30, copyright 1960 Augsburg Publishing House. Used by permission.

Now it is Christ·mas time, Oh, now it is Christ·mas time. Our
Now it is Christ·mas time, Oh, now it is Christ·mas time. Let

hearts are filled with Love and glad·······ness. This is the time of year, Oh,
voic·es ring in ex···ul·ta······tion. Sing·ing in praise of God, Oh,

this is the time of year when joy·ous song will ban·ish sad······ness.
sing·ing in praise of God and Christ, the Lord of all cre- - - - - - - - - - -

a - - - - - - - -tion.

The Happy Christmas

Danish hymn by N.F.S. Grundtvig (text)
  and C. Balle (melody)
Arranged by Harold Heiberg
English version by C. P. Krauth

From *Christmas, An American Annual of Christmas Literature and Art*, Vol. 21, copyright 1951 Augsburg Publishing House. Used by permission.

1. The happy Christmas comes once more, The heav'nly Guest is at the door, The blessed words the shepherds thrill, The joyous tidings: Peace, good will.
2. To David's city let us fly, Where angels sing beneath the sky; Through plain and village pressing near, And news from God with shepherds hear.
3. Come Jesus glorious heav'nly Guest, Keep Thine own Christmas in our breast; Then David's harp string, hushed so long, Shall swell our jubilee of song.

O Christmas, With Gladness

Text by Gustava Kielland
Norwegian melody arranged by C. H. Dale
English version by Melva Rorem

From *Christmas, An American Annual of Christmas Literature and Art*, Vol. 19, copyright 1949 Augsburg Publishing House. Used by permission.

O Christ-mas, with glad-ness and child-like de-light, We all bid you heart-i-est wel-come;
We greet you with jub-i-lant voic-es this night, A-gain and a-gain we say, Wel-come!

We joy-ful-ly clap our hands, We sing with gai-e-ty; So

mer-ri-ly, So mer-ri-ly We turn in a cir-cle and curt-sy.

Wise men from the East, whom we see from afar,
  We know in our hearts what you're seeking;
For we, too, desire to follow the Star,
Your pathway to Bethlehem leading.
We joyfully clap our hands,
We sing with gaiety;
So merrily, so merrily
We turn in a circle and curtsy.

With happiness now I give you my hand;
  Come hasten, and offer your other.
United we are by love's holy band,
We promise to cherish each other.
We joyfully clap our hands,
We sing with gaiety;
So merrily, so merrily
We turn in a circle and curtsy.

Acknowledgments

cover: Consulate General of Finland, New York
2: ©Mittet Foto A/S
6: William R. Eastman III, Tom Stack & Associates
8: (left) The Newberry Library, Chicago; (right) National Museum of Denmark, Copenhagen
9: Picture Collection, The Branch Libraries, The New York Public Library
10: Fred Ward, Black Star
12: H. Fristedt from Carl Östman
13: Fred Ward, Black Star
15: Leif-Erik Nygards
16: Bo Jarner, Pressehuset
18: World Book photo by Joseph A. Erhardt
19: Let Them Eat Cake (World Book photo by Joseph A. Erhardt)
20: Leif-Erik Nygards
21: Lavinia Press Agency
22: Kay Honkanen from Carl Östman
23: Leif-Erik Nygards
24: (top) Leif-Erik Nygards; (bottom) ©Lennard
26: World Book photos by Joseph A. Erhardt
27: Bernard Arendt
28: David Maenza
29: (left and right) Kay Honkanen from Carl Östman
30: Scandinavian Design, Inc. (World Book photo by Fred Weituschat)
31: Bernard Arendt
32: Hollywood Limited Editions, Inc. (World Book photo by Fred Weituschat)
33: Hollywood Limited Editions, Inc. (World Book photos by Fred Weituschat)
34: World Book photos by Joseph A. Erhardt
35: World Book photo by Joseph A. Erhardt
36: Lavinia Press Agency
38: Leif-Erik Nygards
39: Heikki Kotilainen, Lehtikuva Oy
40: (top) Icelandic Photo & Press Service; (bottom) David Maenza
43: N. Göran Algård from International Dias
44: Skane-Reportage

46: (left) World Book photo by Joseph A. Erhardt (right) Norsk Folkemuseum
47: Drawings by Ib Spang Olsen (Consulate General of Denmark, New York)
48: Kay Honkanen from Carl Östman
49: Bernard Arendt
50: Bernard Arendt
52: World Book photos by Joseph A. Erhardt
53: (top) N. Göran Algård (bottom) Knudsen, Oslo
54: World Book photo by Jadwiga Lopez
55: Courtesy of Champion Papers, IMAGINATION XV, Scandinavia
57: N. Göran Algård
58: Nordisk Pressefoto A/S
59: (upper left) Norsk Folkemuseum (lower right) Nordiska Museet, Stockholm
60: World Book photo by Joseph A. Erhardt
61: N. Göran Algård from Swedish Tourist Board
63: Icelandic Photo & Press Service
65–75: John Walter and Associates